BECOMING

A Master's Manual

by

Khit Harding

c 1983 by Khit Harding

ISBN 0-9615868-8-5 Library of Congress Catalog Card
Number: BL624.H317   1986   291.4'3   86-3566

All rights reserved under International and Pan American Copyright Conventions. Printed in the United States of America. Published by Adams Publishing Company, P.O. Box 356, Eastsound WA 98245.

Cover Art and Book Design by Bruce Adams

First printing   1986

The text of this book is based on the teachings of Ramtha the Enlightened One, as channelled by J.Z. Knight, during dialogues held in New York City in 1979 and 1980. It is designed to provide pleasure and information on the subjects covered. Its purpose is to educate and entertain. The author, the publisher and J.Z. Knight shall have neither liability nor responsibility to any person or entity with respect to any loss or damage caused or alleged to be caused directly or indirectly by the information contained in this book.

This is the first volume in the Becoming series. If you wish further information regarding these publications, please send your name and address to Adams Publishing Company, requesting that they be added to the mailing list.

Thank you everyone who contributed to this project.

Thank you J.Z. Without you, my own becoming would have taken so much longer.

Thank you Jeff Knight, Elisabeth Bartlett, Paula Prismon, Harry Lynn, Marc Maislen, Patty Boyce, Donna Webster, Kitty and Bob Hudgins, Deborah Hudgins, Jean Isaacs, Marcia Keizer Batey, Elizabeth Martin, Beverly Dittrich, Pat Jacobs, Jill Kanzler, and Barbara Wood for your encouragement and support throughout.

Thank you Katy Cardinale.

Especially thank you Ernest Kanzler.

And finally, thank you to my wonderful husband for his support and wisdom and love.

This book is dedicated to you.

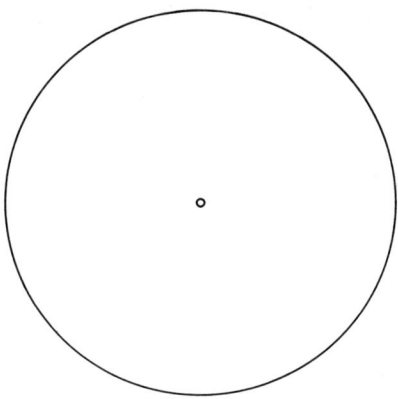

The key to the kingdom of heaven is locked
within you.

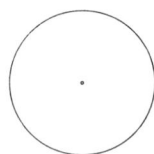

Right within you, sublime beautiful creature,

Right within you.

You are the ideal.

You need not copy anyone else.

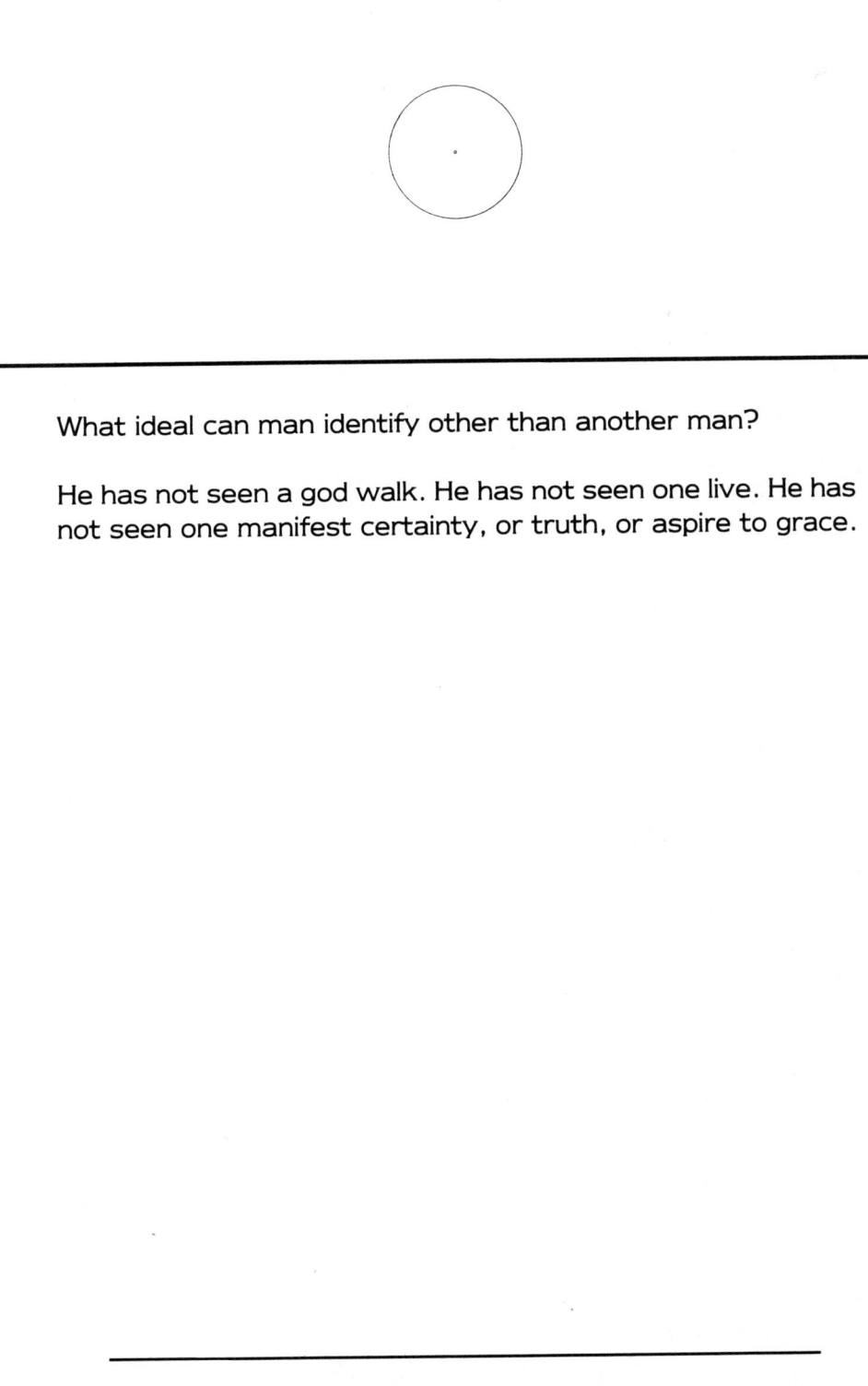

What ideal can man identify other than another man?

He has not seen a god walk. He has not seen one live. He has not seen one manifest certainty, or truth, or aspire to grace.

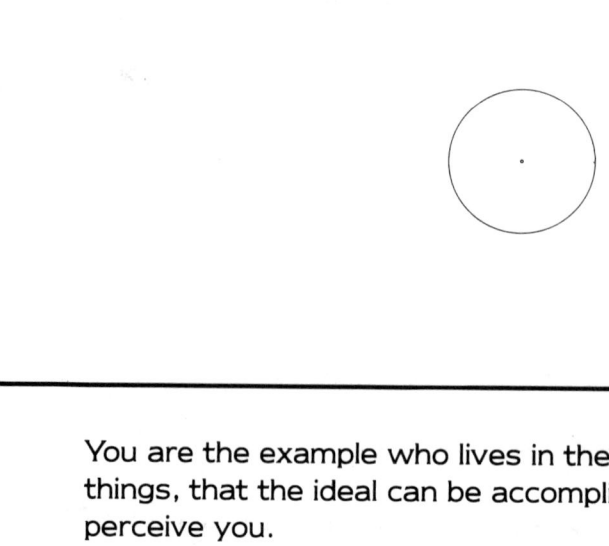

You are the example who lives in the world to do these things, that the ideal can be accomplished within those who perceive you.

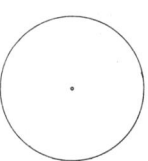

You are chosen to live your light in a world that has no ideal except in heroes of fiction and fantasy. You are chosen to live your light, not as a saviour, but as the explicit god that you are: brilliant, shining, mirthful, happy and manifesting without doubt because you simply ARE.

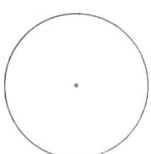

You who are doers in the Source, who are known in all your good, will become a light to the world. You who believe on the principle of BEING, who apply the principles outrightly, who love the Source conclusively will be exalted. You are noble, and your light will be better seen. You will be exalted that your light can be seen by many. That is a covenant and a promise with you.

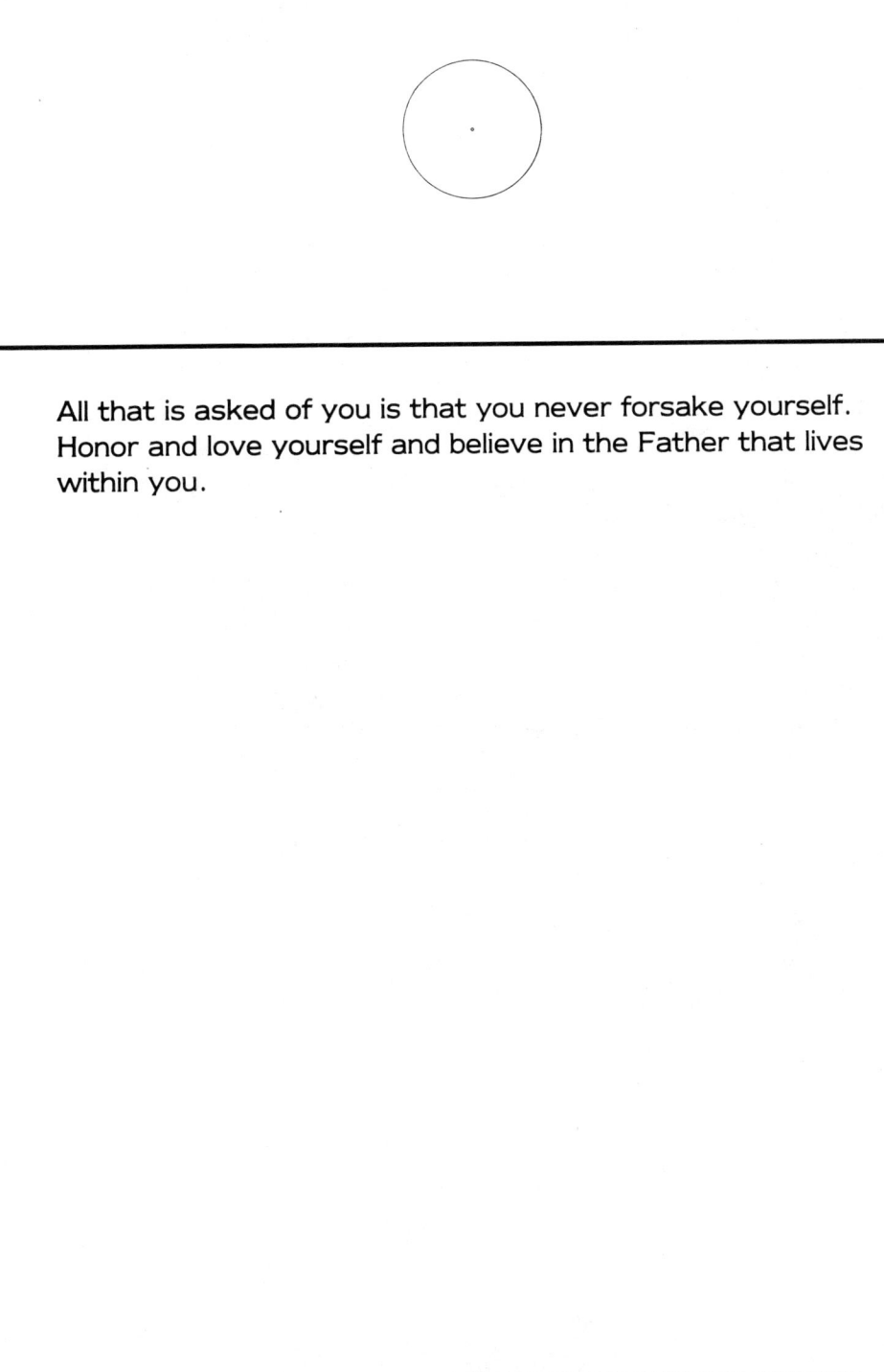

All that is asked of you is that you never forsake yourself. Honor and love yourself and believe in the Father that lives within you.

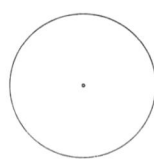

You are the doer of your kingdom. Nothing is ever wasted. All is woven into the fiber of your soul. Life has created a momentous path for you, and always it is remembered and pondered with a light heart.

You learn from all things that are in your way. You learn and overcome and are better for all things. ALL THINGS.

Whatever is in front of you, pursue it to the limit. And when it is gone, create more by desiring it from the Lord God of Your Being. It must come forth.

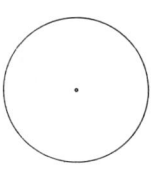

You cannot know how your kingdom can be unless you forsee it and know it. In the seeing and the knowing of it, you already ARE all those things.

○

A wise man will go outside of his province and take a grander view of himself and all he sees, yet few do this.

Those who do are wise men. They are the masters. They are the truth and they are the light.

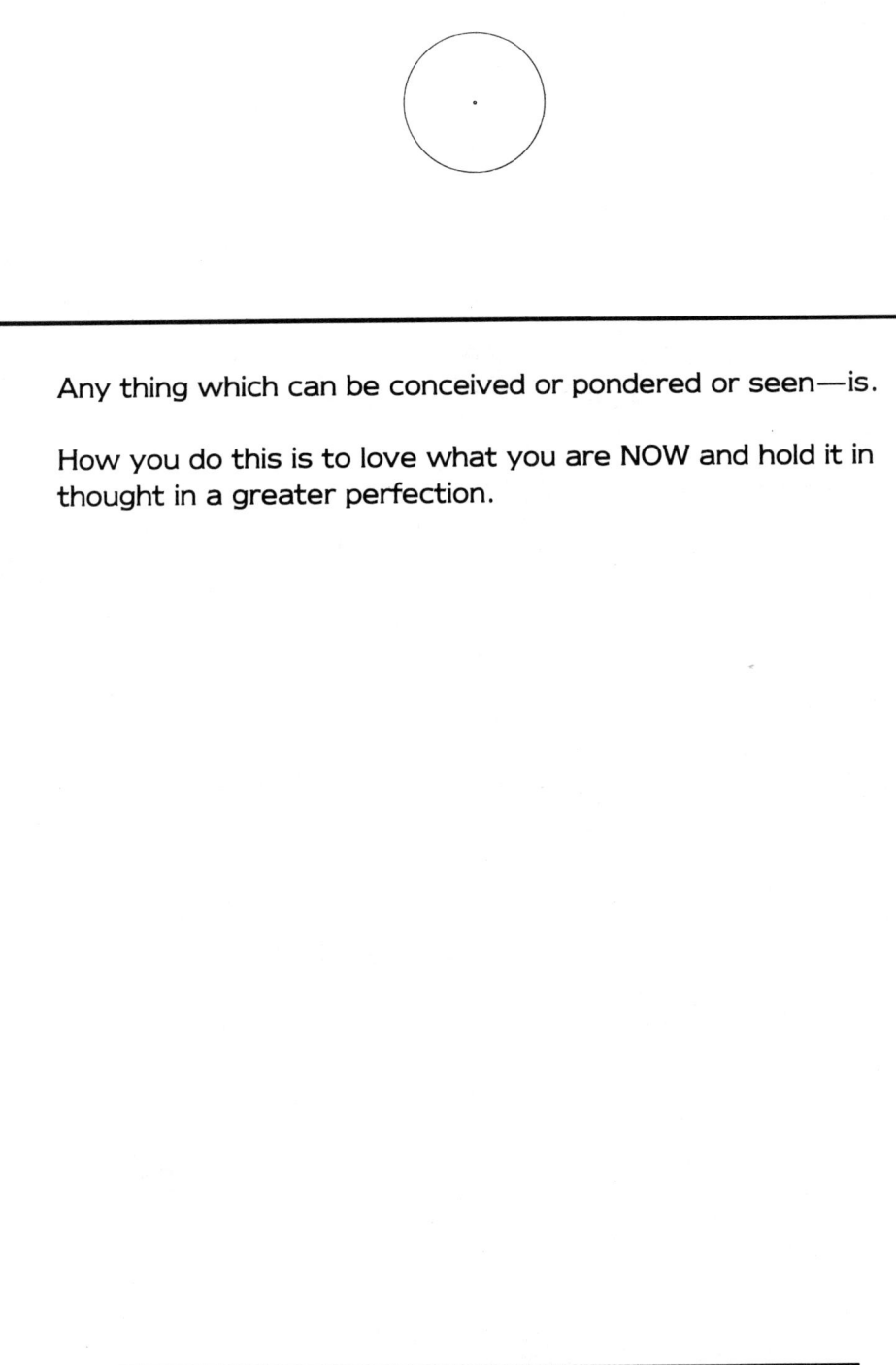

Any thing which can be conceived or pondered or seen—is.

How you do this is to love what you are NOW and hold it in thought in a greater perfection.

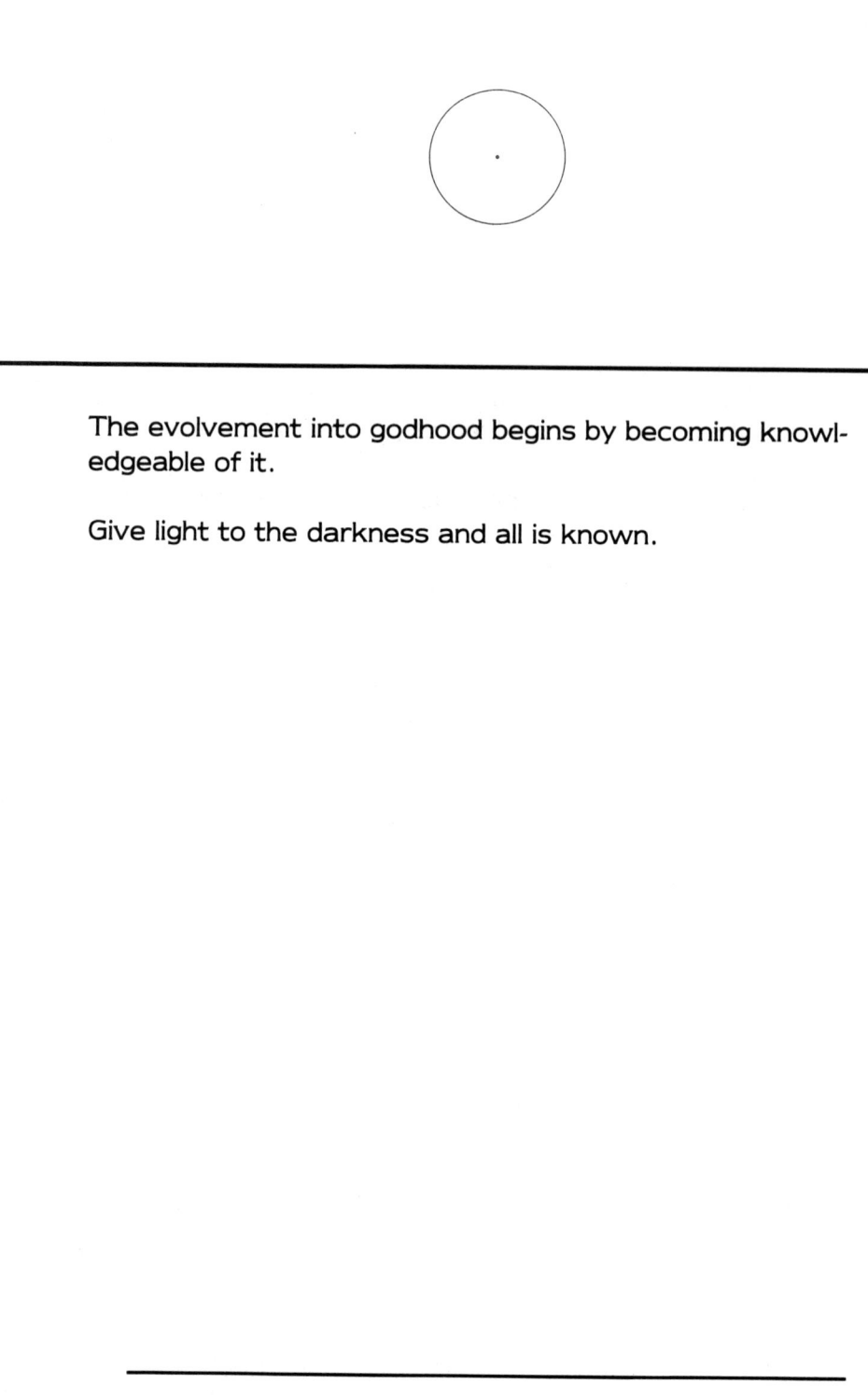

The evolvement into godhood begins by becoming knowledgeable of it.

Give light to the darkness and all is known.

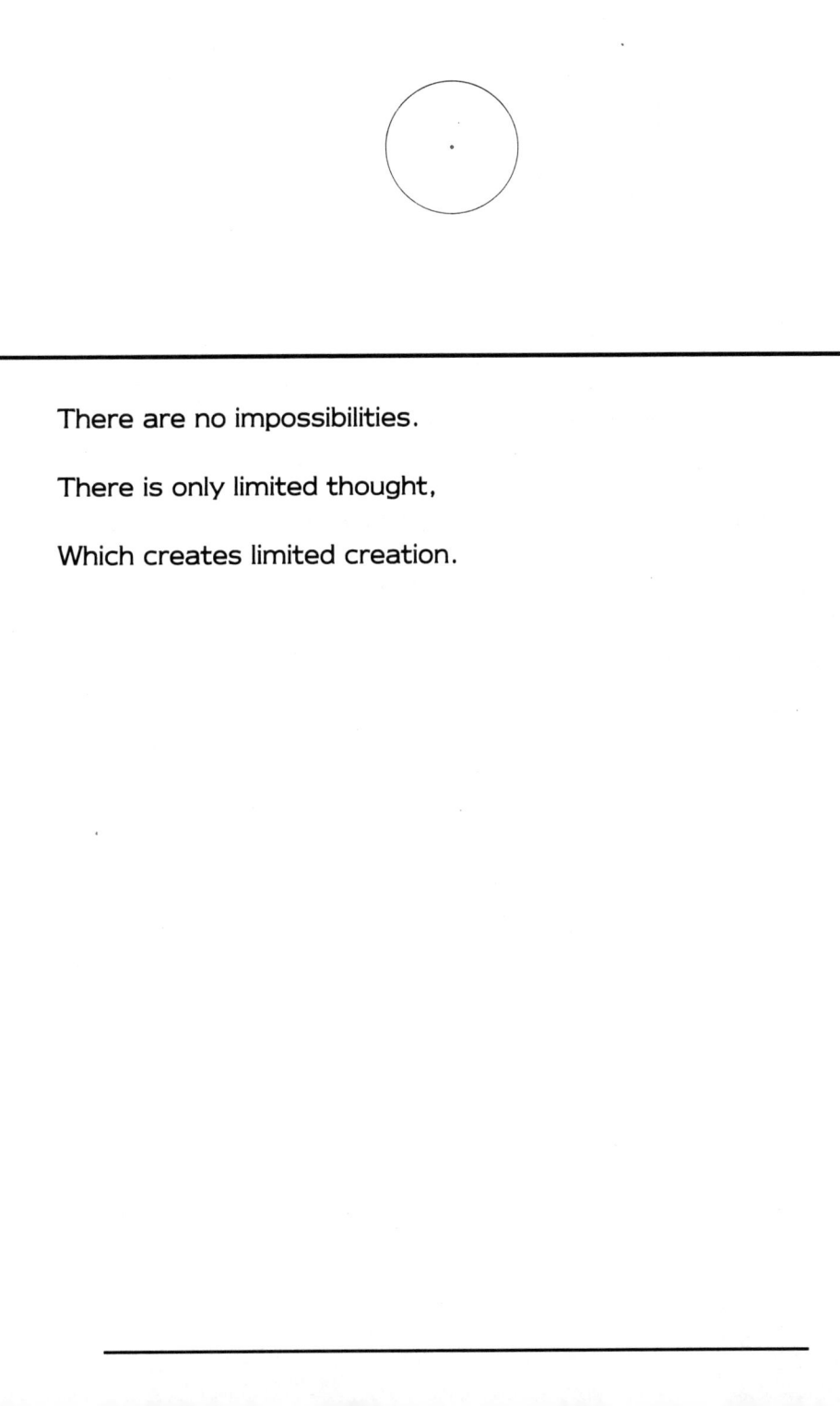

There are no impossibilities.

There is only limited thought,

Which creates limited creation.

It is how things are seen in attitude that determines their measure and their beauty.

See ugliness and seek the beauty within it.

That which is ugly has beauty within it, for all things emanate from God sublime, thus if something has presence, importance and value, it comes from the Father and He is beautiful.

Find God in all things in a more refined manner.

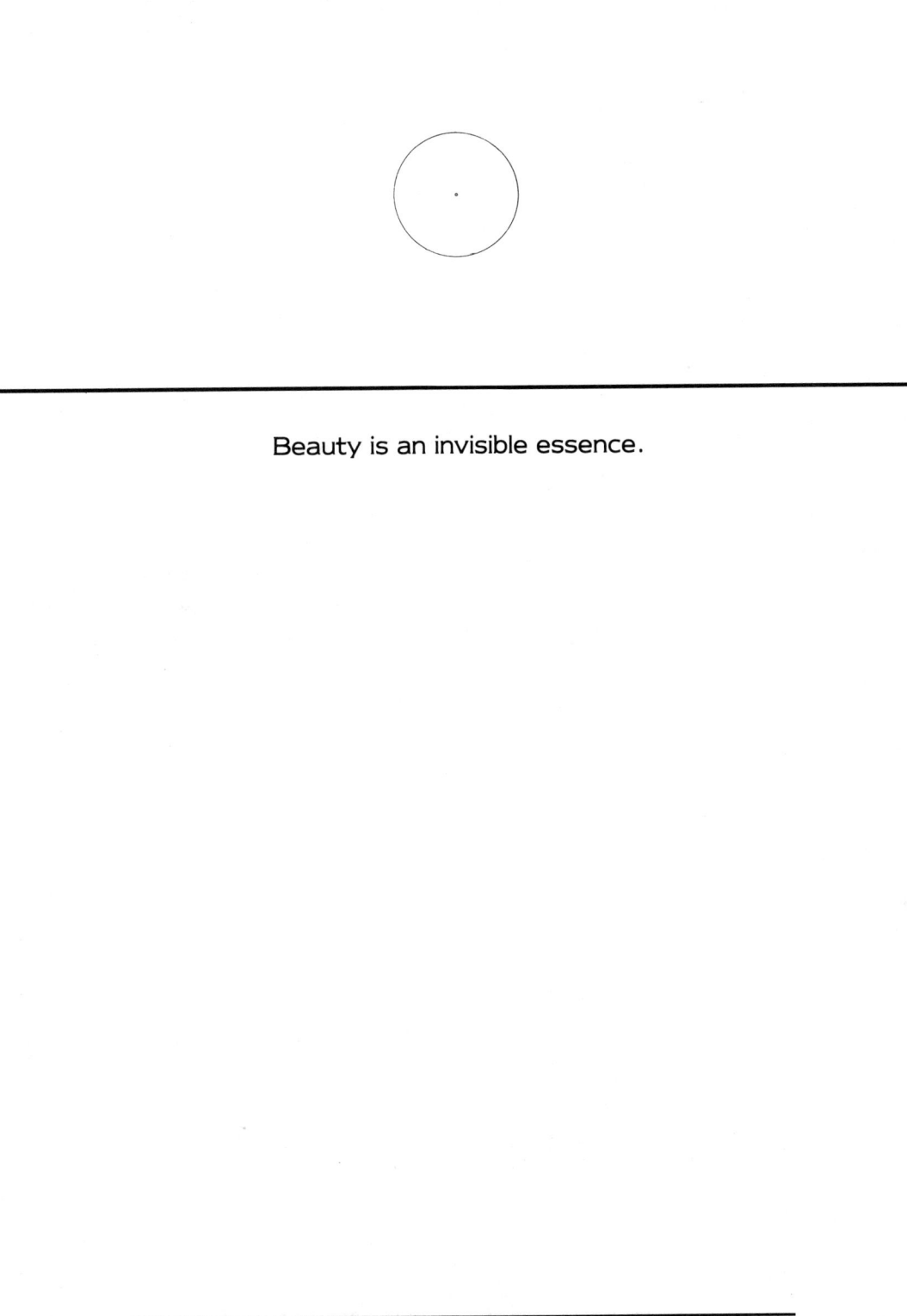

Beauty is an invisible essence.

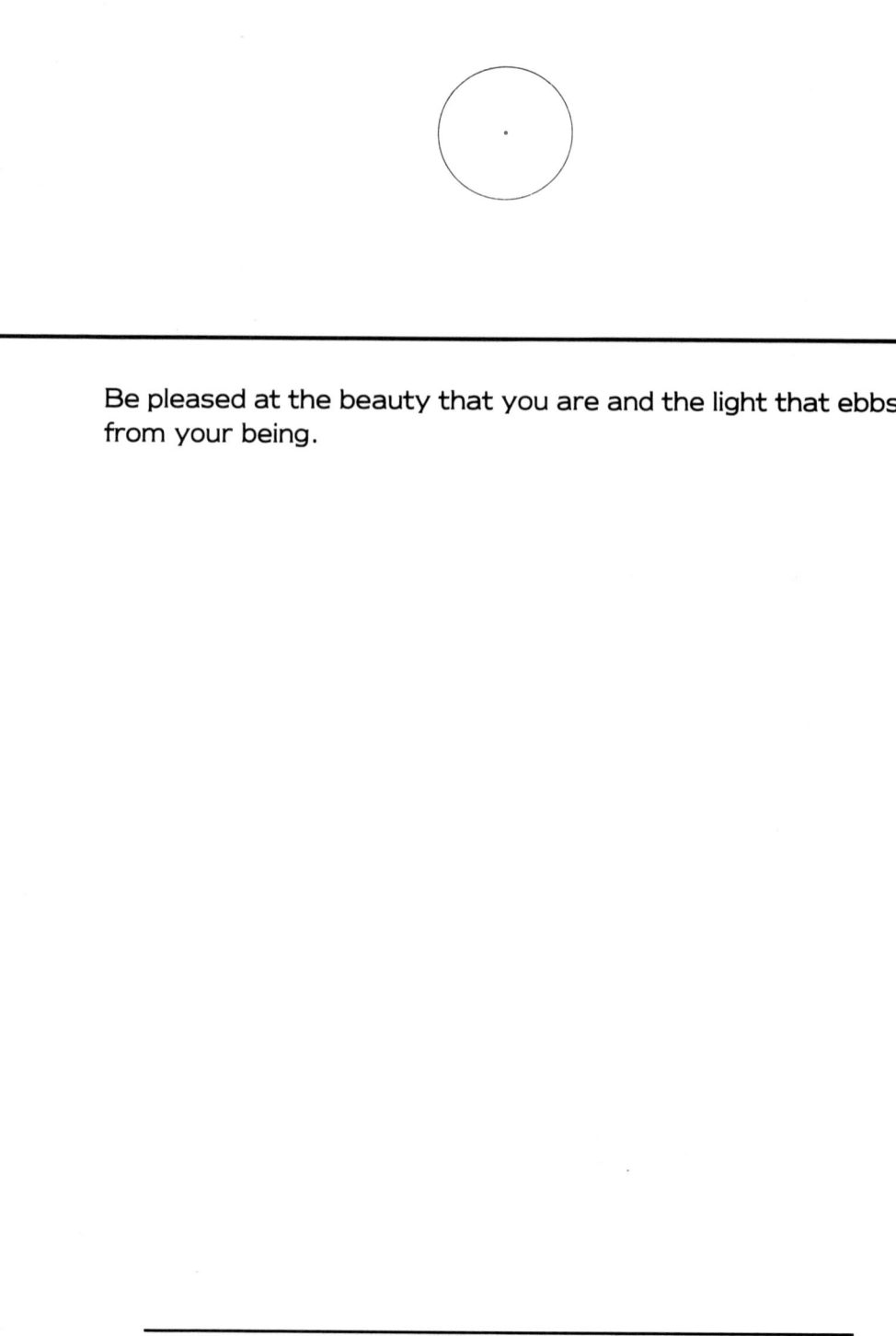

Be pleased at the beauty that you are and the light that ebbs from your being.

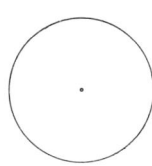

Never be disappointed in being you, for you are divine and glorious.

Never underestimate your beauty, your might or your heritage. Your heritage is steeped in the stars.

You are forever.

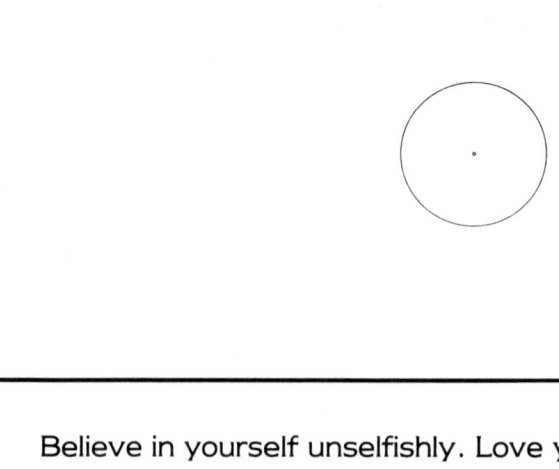

Believe in yourself unselfishly. Love yourself conclusively, for this is the true prayer of God Almighty and is, in all understanding, the greatest way to live His light as yours.

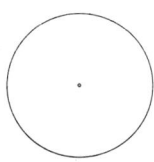

Let your light shine forth into life.

It matters not where you are, but how you are BEING wherever you are.

Light is continuous.

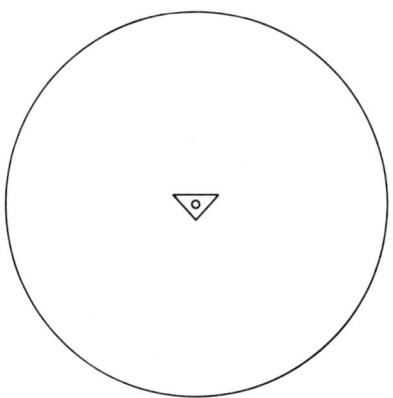

When anyone asks you "What is the source of your beauty, your happiness, your success?" answer, "It is the Father within me that does all these things."

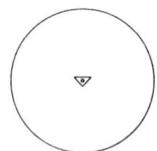

The Father's request, and all that He is, is simply this:

I have provided forever, continuum. Live it as you will, but be happy. Live this life as you will, but be happy and joyous. And love life.

Love life, and participate in it readily, for it is a gift from the Father.

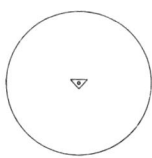

Few expect God to be simple, but He is all the sweet and simple things of life.

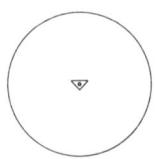

God is the little boy's face. If you look clearly and simply you will find this truth wonderfully so.

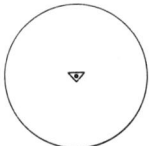

God is the joy of seeing a desire completed, of seeing a manifestation become a miracle, of seeing an error in judgement through a desire and seeing oneself gain through it.

He is all life.

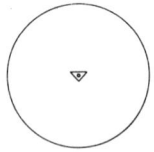

How do you love God?

You live Him.

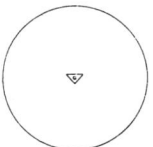

Speak like a god.

Love like a god.

The shadow you cast is remebered by those coming up in the rear.

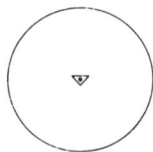

When you speak as God, the aqueous substance listens.

The void responds.

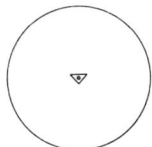

God is living life always in the same light at all times.

God did not evolve from you and become you for only seasons, for only certain times. He is there ALL times.

To master is to become. The greatest mastery, the greatest conquering is to realize this always.

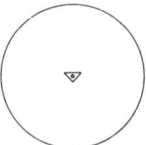

The simpleton in his compulsive contemplative thought can reason God and can reason himself. Even the simpleton can contemplate his being. And what is seemingly squalor is really his paradise. The Father is known to him as the Father is known to the greatest kings.

The Father is for all people.

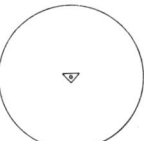

You are the saviours of yourselves. You are the dictators of your own lives. You are the driven good of the good of your lives. You are, in all your simple purposes, God who has revealed Himself in illusions, in hopeful thinking. You are this.

All are the perfect son. You all are the culminated effort of a perfect mind, God, contemplative thought.

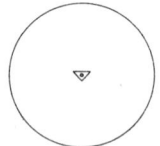

Contemplative thought is expanded thought.

Contemplative thought takes one thought singularily, or one object or entity, and contemplates it, thinks upon it.

You may see and think about many things in your day haphazardly, but to stop and reason with one particular thought expands your understanding, your knowledge and your reasoning in regards to it.

Contemplative thought is the teaching thought.

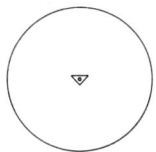

All thinking, all thought, all times—all are thinking continuously, for all are expanding continuously.

Thought is the primal mover.
Thought is the creator.
Thought is conclusively the highest element.
Thought is the Father.

The Christ is the principle of God becoming man. All in One, One in the same.

The understanding is this: all life is God.

Man, God in His singular unique being, is called Christ.

All are the annointed one. All are the awakened one. All are the saviour. All are the Lord. All are the Christ.

A most remarkable understanding.

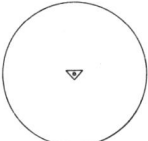

The Christ is the noble son of the Father, the inherited kinship of the Father.

The son is the splendor in heritage that the Father is. The son is readily all the Father is.

The son will accomplish all that the Father will accomplish, and the son will be all that the Father is in all things.

The son is an extension, the perfect part, the extended principle of the Father.

The son is the beloved of the Father.

The son is the inheritance to the Father's kingdom.

The Father knows not life until the son knows life.

The Father knows not joy until the son knows joy.

The Father is to the son all that is.

The Father is to the son all that is seen in life.

The Father is to the son honor, respect, the action of these words, the ideal, the purposeful being from which he sprang.

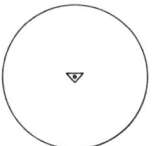

The son is to the Father all good, love, all joy, honor, purposeful being.

The son became Christ, the realized form of the Father, that he might see and understand all of these things his kinship has prevailed upon him.

One entity can change a universe if he knows he is a Christ.

There are whole nations of people who believe that one entity will save them all.

All are Christ. The prophecy of the return of the Christ is the return of the Christ seen in all people. That is the true prophecy.

When all realize that God, Supreme Life, Power Divine IS them, when they truly realize it and know it in their beings, then Christ is risen.

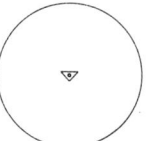

The Christ in man is realized when man begins to contemplate himself as the Father has contemplated Himself in the birthing of His beginnings. When man contemplates himself, he extends and expands himself, and behold, it is a truth, a wondrous thought: the creativeness that has aligned itself with the co-crativeness of the Father comes into perfect view.

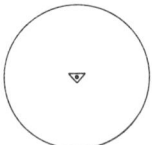

Christ is God living, the Father.
God is Man.
Man, being the lower form of his own creative thought, becomes splendid God.
To attain the kingdom of heaven is to simplify you and God.
The Father is as the simplicity of the light.
To come to His kingdom, one comes with the sweet virtue of simple thought.
Simple thought permits pure reason.
When the vortex is closed, the Father has taken outward from the being and seen inward from the being.
Then, behold, there comes into this third dimension, great and joyous peace and life of a most splendid kind.

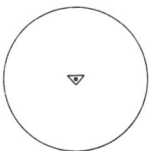

THE LORD GOD OF YOUR BEING

The Lord of your being is the soul of your being, the divine memory. All words, all actions have lodged themselves within the Soul. It is a record of sorts, thus it is the Lord of all your being.

The God of your being is your light body; its first perimeters; the mass known as thought. It is the evolvement of God through expanded knowledge. It is your first embodiment, your light.

These are centrally focused to come forth through the ego of your Being.

Thus you are speaking from the Lord God of Your Being.

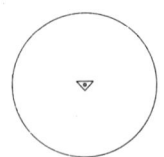

FROM THE LORD GOD OF MY BEING
I CALL FORTH MY CHRIST
INTO LIGHT,   INTO LIFE,   INTO NOW.
SO BE IT.
FROM THE LORD GOD OF MY BEING
I CALL FORTH MY POWER:
COME FORTH,   NOW.
SO BE IT.
FROM THE LORD GOD OF MY BEING
I CALL FORTH MY KINGDOM:
COME FORTH PERFECT,   NOW.

SO BE IT.

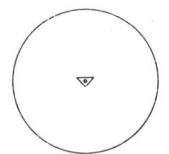

BELOVED FATHER:

ALL THAT YOU ARE, I AM.

BELOVED FATHER:

WE ARE ONE AND THE SAME

NOW AND FOREVER.

BEHOLD UNTO YOUR BEING YOUR PERFECT SON.

BEHOLD UNTO YOUR BEING THE CHRIST

THE SON GODMAN

NOW STANDING FORTH

NOW AND FOREVER.

ALL MAY KNOW

I AM THE LORD GOD OF MY PERFECT BEING.

ALL MAY KNOW

I AM THE CHRIST,

NOW AND FOREVER.

SO BE IT.

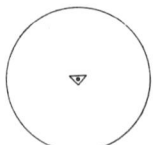

The new age is termed the Age of God, the Age of Spirit manifested into the Age of Light.

All things are powered through light. Light is that upon which subsequent thoughts are carried.

Times as you know them shall be no more. Governing as you know it shall be no more.

The principle of the Life Force shall prevail.

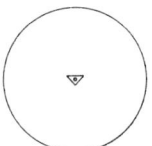

All that are warriors of the old laws, all that are conquerors of the old laws that have enslaved people—their days are finished.

Behold, there shall come forth a great shout. It shall come from the soul of man, for man, who has lived under the tyranny of threatened law, will be free.

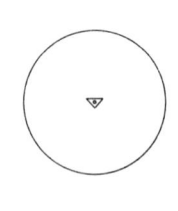

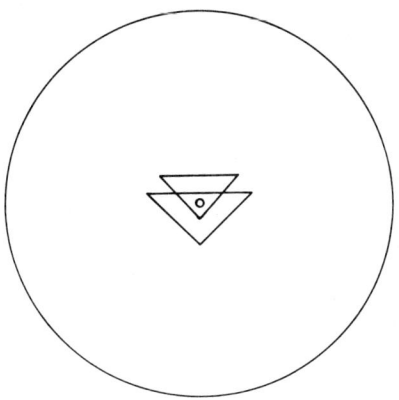

ALL THAT YOU WANT IS YOURS.

But you must do away with the illusions, the struggles, the games that keep you from getting it.

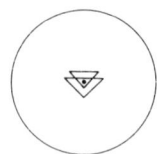

Do you know what illusions are? The things which make you UNhappy.

That is the illusion.

Removing that from your sublime existence, you can get on with manifesting glory; desiring and doing all the things that you wish to do, happily.

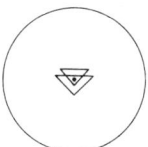

Being God is being this life happily. HAPPILY.

To peel away the illusions that hide the distinctive God within you takes courage and the wonderful will of want: TO WANT TO. That is when walls can be torn down to allow you to walk through, and universes can be split to provide you a better view, if you wish.

But it does no good unless you want to.

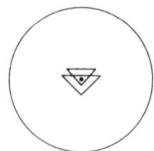

Become the Lord God of Your Totality and peel away each illusion that inhibits the magnificent creature that lies within you, that you can be a light to the world.

God is simply a collection that is everyone, seen and unseen, each of you. God is a greater strength that lies within, that is clear and shining and bright and everlasting. And for you to know love, you must remove those things that forbid you to see it.

You think you are loved because of your face, because of your tresses, your linen, your labor, your manhood, your womanhood?

You are loved for that which is the supreme Source, that which is within you. And to that Source is acknowledged the illusion you wrestle with continuously. You are a fine delicate instrument which allows the seat of God to reign in your dominion.

Many of you are reaching for your fortunes and successes and you will have them. You MUST, for your soul drives you to do it.

But never forget God, the Source, first and foremost, beyond all that you get.

And never lose sight of that which is within. For in the days to come, it is from within that strength will be drawn and light will shine forth.

You will be known by that which you live, that which knows what it is.

You will be the connector—this has all been set into precedence and into sublime pattern.

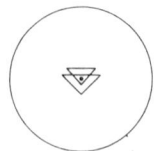

You are going to unfurl the standard called the Lord God of My Totality: I AM. I AM. You are going to reach beyond illusions that lock and bind up the sacred soul, the sacred light. You are going to find that your light is going to transcend into a brilliant array of colors and that it is going to become more visible.

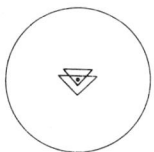

You have to know who you are and what you are.

GOD.

It is a very simple explanation.

Burn your calendar. If you look you will see no calendar in the blue sky, no clock in the water. And if you look to the wind to tell you what time it is, it will blow your hat off!

Live for the moment. Life is in the moment. It is not within time. Time is the destroyer of life. Time is what makes you grow old. Time is what takes your youth away. Time is what takes your bones and makes them dust.

Enlightened people will not be enslaved by the illusion, the enigma of time. It is such a reality it is an unreality.

Can you reach out and touch an hour?

Live your moment as it comes. When you do your projections, your projections are meted out NOW. Their fulfillment is in the now. The now. The Now. The NOW.

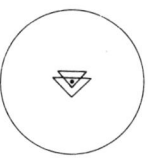

Your lives are a whisper in time to those who live in forever.

Do not try.

KNOW.

What you FEEL is what you know.

God is emotion.

Indifference is being without emotion. When you are indifferent you are without emotion. You are not seeing your divinity, for God is emotion.

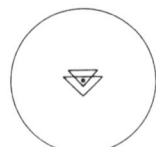

Emotion is not born of the body. It is explained in the body through spasms.

Emotion is born of gratified thought, felt in the person and expressed in the body; becoming lightness, humility; feeling love, deep feeling; often a weeping soul that knows not why it weeps; tenderness, gentleness, compassion.

You are happy when you are fulfilling your destiny.

Happiness gives you youth.
Happiness gives your soul laughter.
Happiness gives you smiles
Where once you knew sorrow.
Happiness gives you contentment in change.
When happiness is found,
Love is found,
Peace is restored,
God is seen.

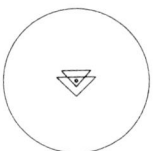

Everyone needs to be without the worry or concern of gold. Everyone may have gold as long as gold is not the priority, happiness is. Everyone. Then we have people who are joyfully free, for they do not labor for the pence, or the ruby, or the drachma, but for happiness. They are doing that which makes them happy. Then they are secure.

There are great kings whose wealth you cannot even imagine, who are looking for happiness.

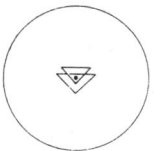

A kingdom can be great

When there are no kings,

Only free men.

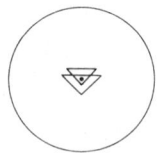

COME FORTH DIVINE SOURCE,

INDEED WONDROUS FATHER:

BRING FORTH TRUTH

AND THE GLORY AND THE POWER

TO MANIFEST

FOR THE FATHER

WITHIN ALL.

SO BE IT.

There is no greater truth than you.

You are the product of your desire.

You will live forever.

It is how you desire that will make your life happy.

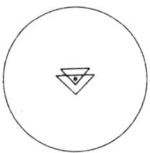

When desiring, simplicity is the most direct line to God.

When you see everything as God sees it then

it is all yours.

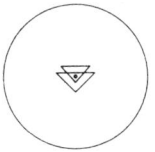

As soon as you let go, things are attracted to you through naturalness, not through need.

Whatever you want you will get.

You can never exhaust the supply.

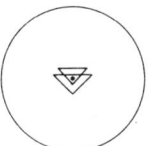

You have to have an allegiance to the desire in order to make it manifest. The moment you desire it, it already IS, for the ideal pattern has been set. It is following through in the acceptance of it that makes it manifest. It is the acceptance of it that brings peace.

A master says: "It already is."

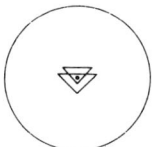

You enslave yourself for things, and most of the things are unseen, unfortunately, like future. A day will come when none will have to work for the other.

When a master becomes a master he does not toil in the field. The bread is manifested before him. He does not go into the marketplace to purchase a meager humble wool for his shoulders with some pence he has earned. He manifests it for himself. That is the priviledge of being a master. That is why it is worth becoming a master. That is why you should put all you have into making yourself great.

You should put yourself in such a place that greatness will surely come without the inter- action or interruptions of those who would limit you or enslave you.

What is it that lives forever? Is it not your beautiful being that created the very adornment that is upon you? And what do you cleave to so tightly? Things that you have created. It is better to cleave to yourself. Then you have all the kingdom.

It is good for you to wonder to what extent you can overcome your fears, to understand to what extent you can become yourself. It is good for the soul.

What is good for one, all have. None is greater. None is less. All are the same. The Father is no greater than any singular person. He is not less. Thus, what one possesses readily, all possess readily.

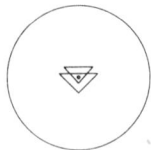

God takes care of you by letting you make your own decisions, which He is.

You must discern what it is you need, want, desire. Only you know what is best for you.

When you have decided what you want to do and by loving yourself, have allowed yourself to make the decisions, then the door will open for you, straightaway.

You must discern what you want. That is how it is here in this third dimension.

You are not given any one thing unless you ask.

When you ask the Father within you, the Father within you becomes a live embodiment and restores peace and balance. He is the restorer of life. He is the giver of life.

And when you ask enough of the Father, and bless the Father within you at all times, then the Father within you becomes you through the acceptance of your attitude, through the acceptance of your being.

Then, no longer do you have to ask for anything. For your mere thought is answered by the Father within you, for He is the one doing the thinking.

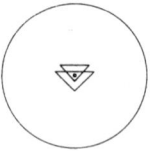

It is difficult for doors to open when they are locked from your side.

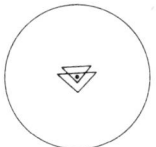

A law is a limitation.

The truth is unlimited freedom.

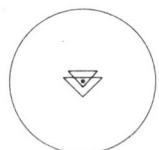

The sovereignty of man needs complete freedom to express, not as radical movement, but as man's individualized God-self-will in accord with his sovereign kingdom, which is his life.

The explicit purpose of Man is to become God in His silent awakening and to live God unrestricted in co-creativeness with His own design.

Others can give you advice and always you listen. But you must learn to assess it in your own kingdom.

If anyone takes you and replaces you according to his schemes and designs, and tells you, "You must be this, and must do that, and must follow this law and this regulation and this writing, and this and that, and that and this", then you are not a sovereign god and a sovereign man—you are man the rabble. You are man the slaughtered sheep. You are not the shepherd.

You do not have to take into your kingdom any thing or person or power if you do not wish to and if you are not aligned with it.

You may accept and love it in the truth that it is. But never forget the truth that you also are and let that stand.

Learn to be you at your own will, and govern your life according to you. In the final analysis, only you have been responsible for all your actions, thus you have departed from guilt and responsibility and enslavement in the entrapment of the emotional feelings of those who care for you.

So be it: Man the sovereign.

Know who you are by experiencing it. When you find yourself, you will find that you are the genius of your own creativity.

All have participated readily in all creation. When you go back into that memory, the attunement returns to you also. Then you can apply whatever uniqueness you have to individualized creation and it becomes an extension of your being.

You may create however you choose and for however long you choose. You go back into the Father. You go back into creation. You go back into the evolution of life continuous You go back into being that which you are in a more perfect state and you can create from a more perfect state.

You can choose to create whatever you desire and you will succeed.

You are caught by thoughts and by remembrance.

You separate yourself with objects that remind you of past memories. The strongest reminders are those of metal.

If you have in your possession any one thing that reminds you of sorrow, or perhaps a lacking of worth, you should rid yourself of it and go and buy another thing.

Records may be closed to the past, but not memory, reckoning, or thought of it in the present moment. You experience a thought, or even the action of another, and see it, catch it again in thought.

It is simple to overcome. Instead of seeing these things, look closer and see the Father in the being.

You can always go past the illusion into a greater depth of reality if you will see the good when you look there.

When you become the thought, the thought will manifest readily whatever you think into pure thought, which is the elevated substance of gross matter, the first plane as it is seen and known, the third dimensional plane.

If you want to do this, do it with no memory, and pursue the memory to come.

Do it.

You can.

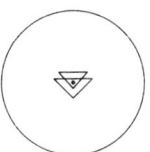

When you see purposeful good, completed good in all things, and you see yourself purposefully good in all acts, thoughts and deeds, then you are good at doing all things in which you partake. Then failure becomes a no thing, for you can never fail in your eyes, and ultimately, that is where it counts.

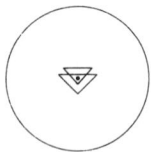

In order to properly assess any decision or person, ask that the mask come down.

One can truly see, beyond the mask of illusion and purported emotion, what lingers behind it.

If it is to the good, then partake of an exchange. If it is not, you will know the truth to make a good decision for your life.

If there are no answers, it means you have

overlooked the obvious.

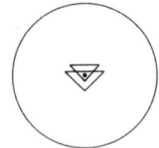

When you are ready to let your light radiate without needing an audience, then

        you

                are

                        really

                                a

                                        star.

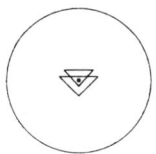

ALL GREAT THINGS THAT ARE EVER ACHIEVED

ARE ACHIEVED IN A LIGHT HEART.

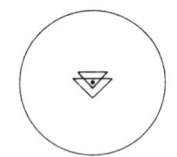

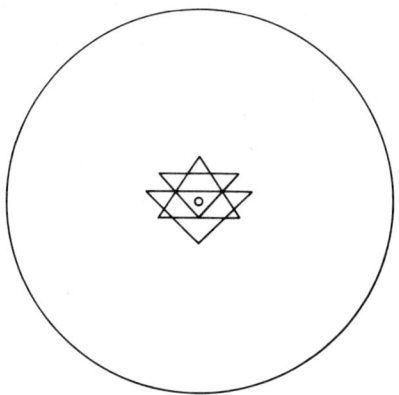

You cannot be a god and not love ALL of what God is—man or woman—and understand these processes and how they were formulated in their perfect order.

Love in the ultimate form is the love of the Father for all that He is. He cannot be without Him and you are not without Him. Thus you are permitted to be your own design, which is Him. That is the love innately at the root of your being. It is the root of life.

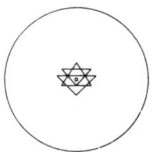

Love is a sacred word. The love that woman has for man and man has for woman co- represents itself as man's love for his God, for when man loves his God he creates. When woman loves man, they create.

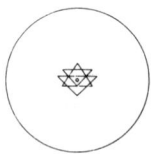

The hue and sweetness that is seen in the eyes of lovers is the sweetness that is seen in the mind's eye of the Father for you. It is a grand and wondrous thing. It does not represent copulation. Copulation represents a part of love. It is the creation of love.

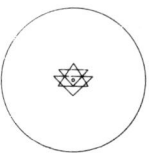

Men and women are separate in their beings, expressing their emotions according to their gender.

God is woman and man. He is the attitude steadfastly within His being.

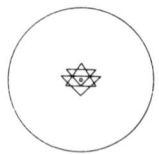

When man sees in the eye of woman the tenderness in her heart, her loving ways, the sweetness about her, he is seeing an element that he possesses in the inner root of his own being, yet does not readily portray in his lifestyle or in his form of being.

He loves it and it is good for him. It is honey.

Man wishes to possess woman for her understanding, her attitude, the current of her electrical field. It completes him.

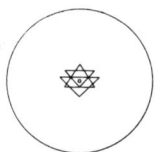

Woman, in her gentle way, sees strength, nobility and honor in men.

It is difficult for women to love men without honor. Honor grounds men and gives them steadfast ways in which to express. It secures them.

When women love honor and strength and the ability to be robust in character, then men can be heros, for women are the gentle beings which men find at the root of their own beings, seen and expressed through the eyes of that which they love.

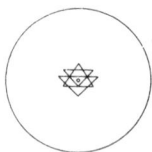

It has been in the nature of women, in the society in which you live, to be leery of self-seekers who will placate their virtuous bodies, take from them that which is admirably termed respect, and give them only an empty bed and a longing heart. To have anyone care for them, was only to care for them at a price. To give up their intelligence to become a kept woman was an abomination to the intelligence of their beings, and that is understandable.

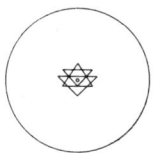

Men, in all of their strength, in all of their nobility and honor, have a great and, at certain times, a grave weakness for the all powerful gender called woman.

Men have gone to war and fought entire nations over the love of a woman.

Men have forsaken their very fathers for the love of a woman.

Men have been prone to do wondrous things and abominable things and stupid things—all for the loss of a woman's love.

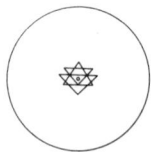

Men in their natures are groomed through their genes to be protective of women, and though they admire the strength of character and intelligence of mind that is free-moving in their women, it is still their innate responsibility to protect them, to keep them, to provide for them, to love and to respect them, the mothers of their heirs. To respect that through the blessed wombs of women, their blood will continue.

Also, it is in man's nature that through his own ignorance he was taught that to weep, or to be understanding, or compassionate, or soft, as a woman is, was unmanly.

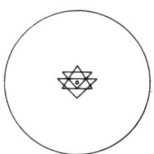

Men in their natures are as women in their softest natures, but the responsibility of continuing their creed, their lineage, their line in humanity has put them, unfortunately, on what is called the battlefield, where they lose their lives for what they love. It has put them out into the market to steal, to beg, to be a part of the rabble, to furnish that which they love with the things they want.

They, unfortunately, are called the rapers of the good, when it is in their natures to have copulation that life can stimulate itself. That is what it is there for.

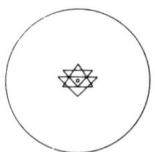

Men in their natures, love beautiful women more than beautiful rubies or diamonds or gold.

The woman is the prize amongst all things.

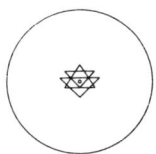

In ancient days a man took a woman and chose the best of the lot for intelligence, beauty and of course, the unexplained emotion of love, to be his virtuous wife, for men were known for their women.

The greatest treasure that a man possessed in his house was not his art treasures, nor his rugs, nor his furniture, his carvings, his draperies, nor his gardens, but the woman who would sit by his side in all her eloquence and beauty.

She was his greatest treasure.

And she was worth dying for.

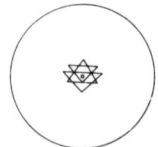

To understand a man a woman must learn to understand herself a bit more, and understand her nature.

In the basis of life they are the same.

It is two genders for the purpose of copulation. For the purpose of keeping the race going on the physical plane there is a separateness, but both are equal.

BOTH are equal.

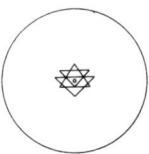

Why do you think that women are born with softer pallor to their skins? They do not have hair on their faces. Why do you think they are born with soft tresses, warm bodies and breasts that formulate themselves erect, bellies that are carved and rounded, and hips that are firm, and legs that are long?

And why is a man, through his handsomeness, merely a mass of straight lines, muscle, tissue, bone and hair? It is better for a man to go into battle not having to heave his breast around his breastplate! And a man has long hair on his legs that when his cloak does not cover them, the cold winter chill will not freeze them, and hair upon his face to grow, to keep his face warm and supple when he is out making a living for the soft, sweet wonder that calls herself his wife.

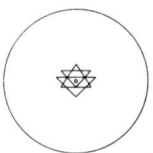

A woman is a prize in a man's heart. A woman's love is a prize to his kingdom, though it is not always outwardly spoken, for it is not in his gender to reveal high emotion, always keeping steadfast.

And though he may try, indeed, in stumbling over unrehearsed softness to explain, or to purchase for her, or to make her life as valuable and wonderful as possible, many times he is often misunderstood.

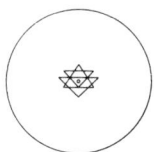

Women have equal say and equal value and equal purpose.

Perhaps women should look at themselves again, strip off all delusions of clothes, look at their bodies and let their bodies tell them what they are.

The body speaks unequivocable truth: their breasts are there for suckling, their bellies are firm and rounded to permit a child to grow within them, their hips are warm and strong to have the ability to move apart and to give birth to a human being, and this cannot be done without the copulation of a man, whose greatest love he can give to any woman is his seed.

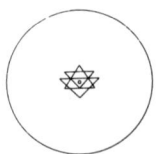

The heart of a man is a noble creature.

He will fight for what he believes in.

He will die for what he loves.

He will give up his own desires to labor to keep that which he has happy.

And that is a truth.

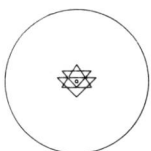

Men are quite content to sit upon their thrones, or their pallets, or wherever their benches are, and be happy in the fundamental clothing that they have, and are quite content with themselves as long as the women they love are happy.

It is in a woman's nature to be a woman and to master fear, whether it is from men, or from ignorance, or knowingness.

It is in the nature of women to love men.

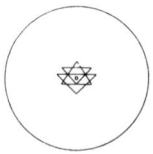

God is both man and woman.

As you experience love and you find it a part of your being, your exhilarated hope is spread to others and soon the exhilaration of hope and the beauty of its profound face is seen in all people.

Then love is shared openly.

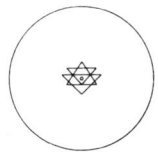

Love is how you see yourself in others.

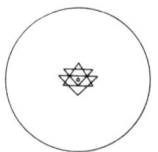

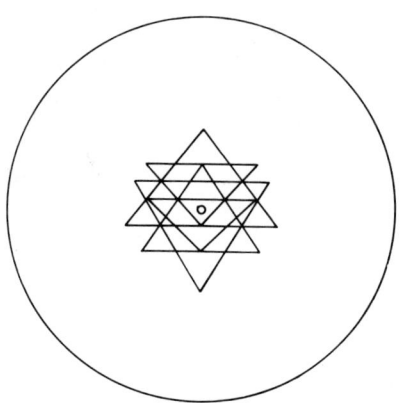

Becoming

Is going

Into the peak

Of being,

Of isness.

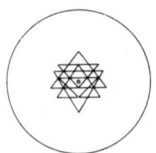

Becoming is the innocence of intellect reversing back to original unlimited Godself, the child, the purity of self.

Then the miracles begin.

Little by little the layers come off, and the innocence that lies within is Divine God, divine master, uninhibited ability, pure spirit, pure genius.

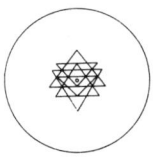

Becoming is emotion—deep profound emotion.

Becoming is the song of ancient knowingness, of gratified now, of glorious future, of reaching for a great star and beyond.

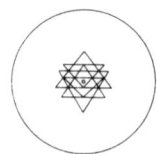

Becoming is feeling. It is love. It is looking lightly upon whatever you see and being at peace with it.

Becoming is removing all fear, for there is nothing to fear and nothing shall ever destroy what you are, for you are pure thought, pure light that can never be taken away.

Remove fear.

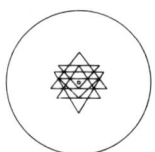

Exault self. Live in the virtue of now. Be glad of a sunrise and a sunset. Laugh with a child and hold it in your arms. See the blooming of flowers. Smell the seasons as they come and go. Be a part of the wonderful enigma of life, and transmute your feelings back in Godhead.

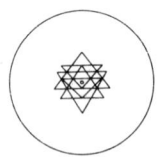

Becoming is unfolding from limitation into unlimitedness.

It is the essence of freedom, the essence of your expression without limitation.

To become unlimited means change, and not all wish to change.

It takes courage to be what you are, but once seen, it is joyous; and it is easier to be a god than not to be one.

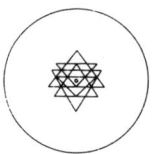

Give yourself the gift of freedom.

Know that you will go on without ceasing.

There is new life in each moment.

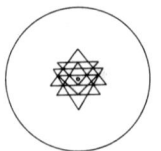

Your task is to change the way of knowing.

Change is a time when limitations are being torn away.

The old is being pulled away to make room for the new.

Change raises you above the ongoingness to another level, another attitude, another perception, but it never retards you or takes you backward.

To understand better, to see more, to expand yourself that you may love and understand and be a helping aid to others, first be all those things to yourself, that you may understand what it means to love and to serve others.

Love and understand yourself without price, without bargaining. When you do, you have expanded a realization of that thought, to a greater concept, and it becomes a permanent reality of your being.

When you love and understand and serve yourself more perfectly, apply it to others. They are drawn to you according to your light.

No one comes to you haphazardly. Each comes for a reason.

When you have expanded yourself through kindness and understanding—not through complexities of intellect, but through the freedom of the simplicity of your own beauty—and given to yourself endlessly, you draw to yourself those who can be taught simply.

Love and understand and help yourself.

Live life by expressing who you are, your truth, your light.

Reflect this not by declaring it, but by living it, and you will be a light to many.

Love the moment. Now. You, now. When you do, you create the desired openings you are seeking. Now.

You will not survive your future until you see and love and are at peace with now.

If you war with your attitude, and are anxious and despairing, you have no future that is fulfilled, for your future is war and despair and anxiousness and uncertainty in the now.

Take time for the sake of your precious being, to find you in all the clutter, and love what you are, rally with what you are.

Then, when you find that you are beautiful, contemplate yourself, and what you will be in foreverness.

The most important, advantageous giver of your future comes from creative thought.

Once the thought is given, the future will open up to you according to your thoughts.

Never lose sight of your ideals.

Know as readily as they are thought, they ARE.

Give thanks to the Father that lives within you for the ideal you have so seen.

Love the moment.

The small wondrous moment.

Many never recognize the moment

Or appreciate its beauty.

Do not seek outside the moment

And you will always gain in your life.

Never be captivated by any thing that inhibits you. Speak forth and reason all things. This frees good things to come into your life.

When you start to love yourself, that is the beginning of all good.

To love yourself attunes you to yourself.

Love yourself that you are in attunement with yourself, that you align yourself with yourself.

Love the God that you are.

Love you.

Worry is a robber of joy and more importantly, life. You worry about something instead of enjoying it, and there will come a time when your worry will be fulfilled. Then you will say, "Where is the joy?".

If people will realize when they have such situations, whether it concerns loved ones, animals, or whatever it may be, instead of worrying about "What if . . ." or "What could be . . ." or "What should be . . ." or "What about tomorrow . . .", they will live and flourish and be happy with the simplicity of the now, they will never have regrets.

It is up to you to decide how you wish to live, how your moments will be counted.

There is an entity that loves you greatly. It is called the God of Your Being. It is your spirit. It walks before you.

Let your spirit teach you. It knows all things. It sees all things, and can give you its eyes to relate to all things.

Let your spirit teach you. Speak to it from the Lord God of Your Being. Have it go before you and let it teach you. It is a grand artisan. Simple. The best things always are simple.

You cannot see anything that you do not first contemplate as a reality. Once you contemplate the reality of it, and whether or not it exists, from that moment on it does exist. Then you have gone into yet another understanding, another adventure.

How can you go into your spirit before you have reasoned that there is anyplace to go?

This is the only way you come into the kingdom of heaven. It is the only way you can achieve God.

Once you know your spirit is there, commune with it and then listen. You have to listen clearly, for your ears are tuned to awkward sounds that represent subtle thoughts.

It is the subtle thoughts you must listen to. Once you have defined your ears so cleverly as to do that, then you ARE your spirit. The more you listen, the more you become. That is how it is done.

In silence of character great understanding can be worked upon your being. This silence is an absence of speech.

Speech is a seductive whore that tempts the heart. It takes your thoughts away and dilutes them.

Be without speech for a period of time that you may be at union with your thoughts. When you are at union with your thoughts, the understanding and wisdom that has a reality in your being will come forth.

In simpleness contemplate your spirit and listen to it. When you do, you contemplate God. He is subtle. Listen to the word that is not a word. See the reality that is not a reality. Become. Now. Be your spirit. There are no doors there, and there are no forbidden walls there. There is not a conglomerate babble nor is there a set of directions on how to become it. It simply is. Live in a state of is.

This third dimensional plane is the test of

fire.

Once the Christ is brought to a seed, he takes all thoughts, amplifies them, and deals with them in the now. That is the reason for the fire.

The fire is a great teacher, for you are at the hand of your own thoughts. If you are God and are now responsible in knowingness for your own reasoning, your own attitudes, what greater teacher than you, the Christ of your being, the God of your being, to bring that into full view so that it may be rectified in the moment instead of waiting as a mar upon the Lord of your being to be balanced at yet another date? The Christ balances it every moment in the continuum.

Bless the fire you go through for the Christ does not prolong karma, it balances it in the now.

Nothing is worth unhappiness. NOTHING.

Be patient with yourself.
Never forget the truth of you:

You are God,
The perfect thought;
You emanate your light
Through the seven planes;
Your beauty is
Inevitably to return
To the source of the light.

Close-mindedness, the atrocity of limited thought, is the one thing that keeps you from your perfect kingdom, keeps you from the glory of God almighty and from yourself.

As long as you have limited thought, cloistered minds, you never adventure into the unknown or speculate or contemplate its existence for fear it means change.

And certainly it does, because there is more now to contemplate, to view, to understand, to be a part of than there was before in a tidy world that lives and dies.

There is coming a day when you will enter into another kingdom—all of you. When all your illusions and your games and your interactions with death and all things terrible and good are played out in the spectrum of karmic rule however you would have them.

When all this is finished, you will come into another kingdom and be the ever-present, ever-continuing glory of life sustained and earned and learned through the enigma called life and illusions.

When ALL realize that the Father, in the beauty that He is, is THEM, then behold, to this kingdom, this place, will come life lived honorably, peace, and joy issuing forth on a grander scale in a grander perfection.

When ALL realize that they are God, they are no longer enslaved, they are free. Free to express, not in the grabble that has given them limited thought and enslavement, but into the extension, the purposeful end that is called FOREVER in God's eye.

All are free to come up into the light of their beings, into their hopeful parts. All are the peacemakers. All are the saviors of their beings. All are the Lords of their beings. All are the lawgivers of their beings.

All are free.

The truth is that all things are true.

All things are God.

Not just a select few are chosen for this message or annointed, ALL are annointed. Soon all will realize this.

Nations will not be separate. Creeds of people will become one. Nationality and races—all are beautiful, all are unique, for they express the beauty of the Father, and joy shall ring forth.

It is the new heaven.

Blessed is Life who permits this to be.

Blessed is the Father who understands perpetually.

Blessed is the Soul that is earnest.

Blessed is the Spirit that never lets you forget.

Blessed are you who are experiencing your illusions,

For one day you will see all

And will understand all;

And the purposeful good of your being

Will reach out greatly to those before you

And you cannot deny your love for them

Or your experience.

Blessed are you, beloved brotheren,

Who will learn to master

Illusions of sorrow and despair

And time that permits this to occur.

So be it.

ALL THINGS ARE TEMPORAL. THE GREATEST LESSON IS LEARNING TO LIVE IN A JOYOUS HEART.

Honor is being who you are and loving the word that represents you and the thought that is you.

In ancient times, the word honor was the cartouche of men in their kingdoms. A man WAS according to his word, according to his thought that created the word.

Statesmen were not known in the land according to papers. They did not need certificates to proclaim they were who they were. They simply were according to who they were, in respecting that and in showing the reality of who they were.

It was called a state of honor.

There were, in times before your history is even recorded, foes who had greater honor than man has on your plane now.

They met in battle and they fought conclusively for the honor that they were, no matter, regretably, to what line the honor portrayed, whether it was enslavement or what else. But they were honorable foes.

What is honor?

Honor brings together the totality of man in his reality.

Honor is an established reality that all men possess and should possess. For if there were no books, or papers, or judges, or lawgivers, or laws to be governed by, how could an establishment in the core of its society live and be governed? How is it done?

Through honor.

There are those of you who give your word, that the word represents the totality of your being, yet you never represent the word.

You say to someone that you profess to love him and cherish him, yet on the other hand, you do not assist him, or be there when he needs it.

If a man gives his word that he will assist his neighbor in his need, and gives his word that he will not encroach upon his property to enslave him, then the man is taken for his word and his honor, and peace abides in the sweet valley.

The reason you lack honor is you depend on the law forces and your society to make up your mind for you.

You do not have the straightforward reality of your own being to be a lawgiver and dispenser of the law, and a peacemaker.

Honor.

I honor my being.
I am in reverence to my being.
I love my being completely.
I do not put forth myself
In a direous way,
Unless I am sure of the completion
To which I put forth my body.

Honoring yourself and your word means going through with you word.

You make a promise to anyone that you will do a certain thing. Though you have the right to break oaths, it is true, an honorable man will see his word through.

There are times in your society when it is more of a grateful thing and purposeful thing to complete something for the sake of honor rather than revenue.

The mere fact of the accomplishment can be added to the glory of your self esteem, to your character, to the privilege of being an honorable man.

Honorable men are long remembered. LONG remembered.

They are idealized, they are sought after, they are revered, they are written about, they are spoken about.

Why is it so noticeable a quality that an honorable man should be outstanding in your society? Are so many unhonorable that to see someone expressing brilliantly according to his word is a state of miraculous being, rather than a state of continuous being in the ordinary?

Honor should be the fruitful bounty by which you live your life daily.

When you can stand amidst others and stand on your word and back your word, you will change the thinking of your times and the attitude of your times into what is called the progression into peace.

Peace is a state of totality of God existence. Peace allows ALL to be in peace. Honor permits this to occur. Honor permits the reality of each person to stand forward on his word.

Honorable men think about what they say, contemplate their thoughts, give promises as life, and complete them.

Honorable men are bountiful in trust. They can always be trusted either with the treasury, or your women, or your foodstuffs, or your nation.

Honorable men are this way.

Learn the word "honor" and its meaning— its profound meaning— for you will be honored according to your word. And words and thoughts, in the days to come, will make your reality either a fire, or a heaven.

You will learn to be a god who speaks in the evident freedom of your being, but what you speak is not a passive thought that is given to any listening ears, but words that are truth, that ring forth, that you can stand firmly upon.

When honor is established conquerors are born of their own kingdoms.

Honor permits a man to be in the likeness of his soul, that has urged the completion of the spirit for so long, that brings forth the word of God and its permission to live abundantly.

To honor the Father is to honor the Source. And what is the Source? It is all wondrous things. It is life.

To honor the Source permits you the wonderful right to honor all peoples and their word— that is your only communicative clause with them. It permits you to honor their lives and their freedom, which in turn gives you yours.

Your word: it manifests the Cause.

It is the command.

It is the blessed vibration in tone.

Learn to use it respectfully, whoever you are, whatever you are, whatever your discernments and desires are.
 Learn honor and respect and love at the seat of your being and you will decisively know to speak properly, and in speaking properly, how to maintain the status of discernment in words and thoughts, thus permitting mastery to occur. And honor.

When you honor one another

You truly love one another.

When you honor one another

You love yourself,

The giver of all good.

All of you are conquerors in your own kingdoms, in your own fight for the preservation of will. All are. Though it has been learned eons ago in your time, there is a great way to respect the life of abundance of man, and to respect the ongoing continuance of man and his seed through the word honor.

Learn this forgotten nobility that it represents in your life a god who is centered on the good.

This is the word: HONOR.

In the days to come let honor display itself remarkably to create whatever is needed.

It will come to have you understand honor, to understand the word and its meaning, to understand the god and the total respect of your being that must be seen.

When you speak from the Lord God of Your Being you are speaking from the totality of your thought processes and your desire is revealed.

The Lord God of My Being.

It is an honorable, complete, digested statement. These are perhaps the most honorable words that you can put forth into language, for they hold honor and substance, and will see it through when even the receiver who put forth the desire has forgotten he spoke them.

Honor is a part of this syndrome, this life, this perfection. Let it come forth—honor in all—and see how it is displayed radiantly in your life.

What is left to conquer are the atrocities man has put forth upon the innocence of his soul.

THE KEY TO THE KINGDOM OF HEAVEN IS LOCKED

WITHIN YOU.